CLASSICAL
PIANO SOLOS
COLLECTION

VOLUME *NINE*

Wise Publications
London/New York/Paris/Sydney/Copenhagen/Madrid

Exclusive Distributors:

Music Sales Limited
8/9 Frith Street, London W1V 5TZ, England.

Music Sales Pty Limited
120 Rothschild Avenue, Rosebery, NSW 2018, Australia.

Music Sales Corporation
257 Park Avenue South, New York, NY10010, United States of America.

Order No. AM92421
ISBN 0-7119-4498-9
This book © Copyright 1997 by Wise Publications

Book design by Studio Twenty, London
Compiled by Stephen Harding

Printed in the United Kingdom by
Commercial Colour Press, Forest Gate, London.

YOUR GUARANTEE OF QUALITY
As publishers, we strive to produce every book to the highest commercial standards.
This book has been carefully designed to minimise awkward page turns and to make
playing from it a real pleasure.
Particular care has been given to specifying acid-free, neutral-sized paper made from pulps
which have not been elemental chlorine bleached. This pulp is from farmed sustainable forests
and was produced with special regard for the environment.
Throughout, the printing and binding have been planned to ensure a sturdy,
attractive publication which should give years of enjoyment.
If your copy fails to meet our high standards, please inform us and
we will gladly replace it.

Music Sales' complete catalogue describes thousands of titles and
is available in full colour sections by subject, direct from Music Sales Limited.
Please state your areas of interest and send a cheque/postal order for £1.50 for postage to:
Music Sales Limited, Newmarket Road, Bury St. Edmunds, Suffolk IP33 3YB.

Visit the Internet Music Shop at
http://www.musicsales.co.uk

Arabesque No.2 Claude Debussy **4**

Chant Sans Paroles, Op.40, No.6 Peter Ilyich Tchaikovsky **14**

Le Coucou Louis-Claude Daquin **10**

Etude in C$^\sharp$ Minor, Op.2, No.1 Alexander Scriabin **17**

Etude in E Major, Op.10, No.3 Frédéric Chopin **20**

Gavotte 1 & 2 from English Suite No.6 in D Minor Johann Sebastian Bach **24**

Gitano from Impresiones Intimas Federico Mompou **26**

Piano Sonata in E$^\flat$ Major, K.282 - 3rd Movement Wolfgang Amadeus Mozart **31**

Piano Sonata No.19 in G Minor, Op.49, No.1 Ludwig van Beethoven **34**

Prelude No.5 from Six Preludes Lennox Berkeley **46**

Sonatine in A Major, Op.59, No.1 - 1st Movement Friedrich Kuhlau **42**

Arabesque No. 2

Composed by Claude Debussy

Allegretto scherzando

Le Coucou

Composed by Louis-Claude Daquin

11

Chant Sans Paroles
Op.40, No.6

Composed by Peter Ilyich Tchaikovsky

Allegro moderato

16

Etude in C# Minor
Op. 2, No. 1

Composed by Alexander Scriabin

Etude in E Major
Op. 10, No. 3

Composed by Frédéric Chopin

Lento, ma non troppo. (♩ = 100)

22

Gavotte 1 & 2
from English Suite No.6 in D Minor

Composed by Johann Sebastian Bach

Gavotte 2

(Gavotte I da capo)

Gitano
from Impresiones Intimas

Composed by Federico Mompou

27

28

30

Piano Sonata in E♭ Major
K.282 - 3rd Movement

Composed by Wolfgang Amadeus Mozart

Piano Sonata No.19 in G Minor
Op.49, No.1

Composed by Ludwig van Beethoven

Andante

Rondo

Allegro

38

Sonatine in A Major
Op.59, No.1 - 1st Movement

Composed by Friedrich Kuhlau

44

Prelude No.5
from Six Preludes

Composed by Lennox Berkeley